"Shruti Bakshi's poems seem [to come from]
some ambrosial spring with [something]
for all lovers of God. One fi[nds oneself drawn]
by their mystical beauty and [depth.]

Each poem is a love seed coming to life inside the garden of the heart."

- Sri Mooji, spiritual teacher

"Outstanding and elevating"

- Makarand Paranjpe, author and former Director, Indian Intitute of Advanced Studies

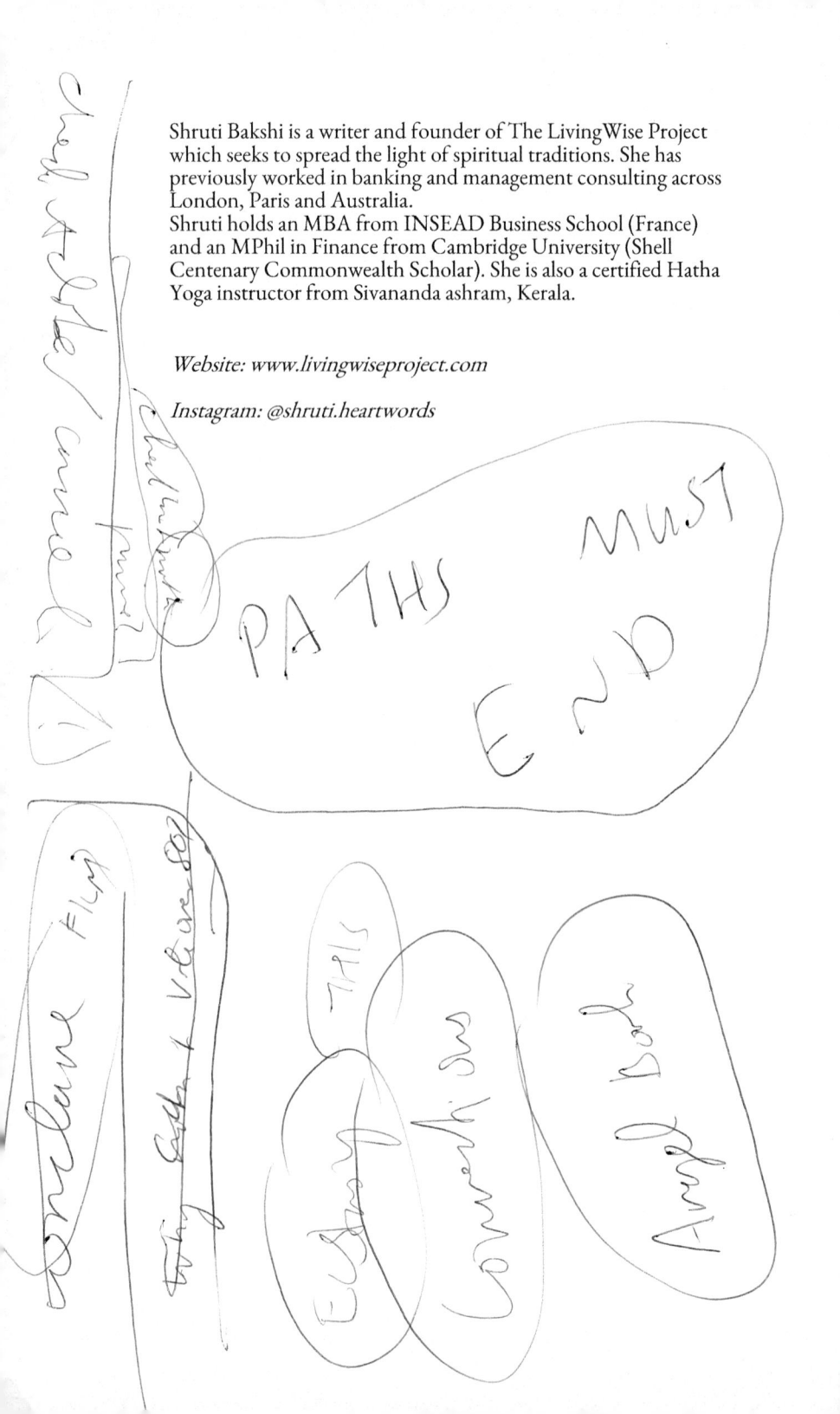

Shruti Bakshi is a writer and founder of The LivingWise Project which seeks to spread the light of spiritual traditions. She has previously worked in banking and management consulting across London, Paris and Australia.

Shruti holds an MBA from INSEAD Business School (France) and an MPhil in Finance from Cambridge University (Shell Centenary Commonwealth Scholar). She is also a certified Hatha Yoga instructor from Sivananda ashram, Kerala.

Website: www.livingwiseproject.com

Instagram: @shruti.heartwords

HeartWords

beauty, Truth, love

HeartWords

Copyright © 2021 by Shruti Bakshi

Second edition, 2023 published by

THE
LivingWise
PROJECT
LWP

India

Illustrations and design by Shruti Bakshi

For more writings, visit:
The LivingWise Project | www.livingwiseproject.com
Instagram: @shruti.heartwords

All rights reserved. This book may not be reproduced in whole or in part, or transmitted in any form, without written permission from the author, except by a reviewer who may quote brief quotations in a review; nor may any part of this book be reproduced, stored in a retrieval system, or transmitted in any form or by any means electronic, mechanical, photocopying, recording, or other, without written permission from the author.

HeartWords is an offering to the fire of Truth, Beauty and Love.

The fire shines Timelessly,
unsupported.
Just sometimes,
some sparks escape,
exploding out of the ecstasy of devotion,
joy of beauty, gratitude for life,…

The words in this book
are a minute and humble expression
attempting to catch some of these sparks
leading Heart-wards.

Dedicated to the Guru for showing the true Life and for His Grace and words that tune the beings to the Heart.

Of those who realise the Truth, a guru is one through whom a dharma flows – a movement of Spirit reflecting divine insight, the ways and etiquettes of Being and carrying with it the power to pull the beings into step with the dance of Existence.

Gratitude to all the Masters

and

to my parents

for the enormous love and freedom

they gave so that I could aspire to find

the truest love and the truest freedom

Saraswati, of wisdom and inspired word

Contents

Krishna   1

Devotion   38

Shiva   65

Love   83

Life   105

Freedom   141

Afterword: On writing

Krishna

KRISHNA

Without Krishna, life is dry, juice-less

What is Krishna?

Krishna is that rainbow glint on the water-bubble
the fragrance of the morning grass
the strike of thunder on a stormy night
the rustling of the trees
and tinkling of the stream

    and sunlight weaving itself into the waves

        to give the optical illusion

            of flashing diamonds

And that morning smell of coffee that warms
your heart as you think of home—
            that we also call Krishna

Krishna is what spins words into poetry
Not the laugh
    but what makes the laugh something we love

HeartWords

what puts the attraction in the touch
what makes life so wanted
    and never lets the daily repeated dawn
        become stale

and that smile that happens in the heart?
    the only one of its kind—
the only thing ever the same for me and you....

that is the most Krishna than anything else

KRISHNA-PRIYA
(BELOVED OF THE IMMORTAL)

What does she want
    the Beloved of the Immortal?
Does she want what the five senses imagine?
Does she want trinkets from the passing carnival,
    the Beloved of Krishna?

The gold and sparkle
of the human dream
can never satisfy
the longing that He does

You can't find Him
in the world of names and forms

The ones who believe everything
        won't believe her;
but in Him she has
        All that is wanted

VASUDEVA

The Lord of the Universe
wants to come and live in your house
    if you accept

He will see through your eyes
He will hear through your ears
He will speak with your tongue
    if you accept
you will have nothing
but the knowing
that He is in you
    as you

HARI

My eyes,
hypnotised
saw one too many

What a trick you play Krishna
to turn from One to many

NAVNEETA-CHORA

Krishna, you would make any mind mad!
But to whom can I complain?

When I separate from your plays,
 separation ends
When I watch your dance, I see that you are
 Still
When I meet you in the most private place,
 I find You everywhere

O Krishna, you would make any mind mad!

But who will hear my complaint…?

SHYAMA

The Shyama of the sunrise has enchanted the
whole world with his dreamy flute

The Shyama of the sunset has bewitched all
beings with his unspeakable dark Beauty

But the Shyama who is beyond
sunrise and sunset—
this One has my full Heart

RADHA-MADHAVA

Radha:
It's fine if you can't love me how I want,
	I'll find another

Krishna:
How many 'another's will you find
	until you find me as all others?

GOVINDA

How can I express
all that He says to me
How to convey!
when He speaks in secrets…

MANOHARA

O Krishna,
I've seen through your trick to make me think
that there is something I need to do or can do
    As if I have ever done anything

Don't play so many tricks on me Krishna
I now live solely on your compassion
If it doesn't exist,
    I'm surely damned

ANANTA

Who will have the courage to save me
now that I have fallen in love
with the One
whose playground
is the whole Existence

KESHAVA

The dark trees stand still with crossed arms
the endlessly black sky offers no respite
I'm wearing out in search of you
not realising you are the Night

GOPINATHA

Who could have made this wayward mind
    understand?
Who could make this body be here
    and take the right steps to you?
Who could make this weak mind have faith?
Who could have even let thoughts of you
    enter my mind?

Now you are caught out, Krishna!
    I caught you out—
and so have earned the right
to live eternally at your feet

GOPALA

It doesn't matter
what you do to me
because
I don't come because you call
I come because He called

It doesn't matter
if you forget my name—
I don't come to build my own
I come in the name of God

It doesn't matter
if you don't love me—
I don't come for your love
I come for the love of Gopal

MADANA

All is old, all is dead, all is past—
let me stay in your everlasting freshness

Pull me out of the graveyard
and let me rest in peace in your Heart,
    my Love

Let me sip from your glass of ecstasy,
let me drink deep the waters of eternal life
let me be in your veins, like you are in mine
without any thoughts;—
    then I am Blessed

ACHYUTAM

If I have left everything that I can leave
    then He Himself must come

If I give up all that He shows me I'm holding
    then He Himself must come

If I'm waiting on His every move
trying to find His breath in the Stillness;
and if all that comes
is a deep cry from the heart

    then He Himself must come

MANMOHANA

All the limbs are heavy with your love, Krishna
all the blood is flowing in your praise
the heart is beating only to remember you
Your Silence quietens the breath
The mind is so drunk on your Beauty
that even myself I forget

I searched for millions of lives
on this earth for you
and when I find you
I can't even express my joy—

Why to speak and put the distance of a word
    between us?

If my mouth speaks, let it speak only your
    Silence

ANANDA-SAGARAM

The pain of separation while I try to understand,
when instead I could be drowning in your Love
The one who stole my heart
and made me useless in the world,
Redeem your own name
as the One who is the last resort
Ocean of Compassion, Infinite Wisdom
and ever-pure Bliss
I'm only hanging by one thread of your
Infinite garment of mercy

I laid all down at your feet
so you would rid me of arrogance
but that very act was such arrogance!
For what is really mine to give to You?

Now my mind seems dumb to itself
talking paradoxes and stunned into muteness
by your Impossibilities

Have mercy for such deluded minds
O great Ocean of Love

NARAYANA

O Krishna
why didn't you tell me
that you are the whole Universe

KANHA

Don't play so many games with me
O Krishna
or maybe you are wondering
like I am too
about how I will bear your Full Beauty

MURALI

The One who is dancing
this magnificent dance of Existence—
all I want is to be the dust on His feet

GIRIDHARI

My mind only finds rest at your feet, Krishna
What will become of me?
My heart finds rest only in the Indescribable
    One
surely I am done for…

O mind,
where are you trying to run all the time?
How can you run outside of God?
Where will you go?

How could you even think to save an inch of
    space for yourself
when Krishna is here?

Surely this is due to lifetimes of delusion
But now delusions are done for;
    the Lord is here

NANDALALA

*'When you heard my call,
why didn't you come immediately?'*

I don't know anymore
if the Dark One asked me this,
or I Him

RADHE-SHYAM

                    I feel in this whole world
                        there's only you and me
Sometimes there's only you
Sometimes there's only me

ACHALA

Your Stillness
sends me to ecstasy

Your Silence overwhelms
my heart with Love

Maybe You're clever
beyond words Krishna…

or could it be
that You really have no idea
what You're doing to me

HeartWords

MUKUNDA

In all my great leavings
there's one thing that never leaves
What a fool you make of me Krishna
when I leave myself
but you don't leave me

DHARMA-MEGHA

Krishna said:
The Gita is my exhale
I Am my inhale
The knowledge is my exhale
Life is my inhale
Wanting to know, you exhale

Keep living, inhale without looking to know
    without looking to get
    without looking for relief

Until it comes by itself
for the two make breath
they cannot "live" or "make life"
without each other

Inhale: "I"
Exhale: "Am"
until they both stop
and you may be as you've always been

Krishna

be hollow
so Madhava can play you

I

never

sang '*to*'

Krishna

Krishna was always the song

Radhé - Radhé

Krishna

MADHURAM

My heart so full of love
is racing to break
Cracked open by the sweetness
that escapes your every pore
Never heard a voice
so fragile-ly pure
yet bursting
with the wisdom and power
of God

Not of this world—
You are not anything
of this world;
Yet to me,
You are all the worlds and universes
Combined

MADHAVA

My backstage Love
is the one I'm thinking of
when the lights come on
and I'm saying my lines

A grand play is happening, I'm aware
but he's not a happening, he's always there

All through the show
I'm remembering his intoxicating fragrance

when the curtains fall
I'm filled with Him

SHYAMASUNDARA

Even Krishna can't be counted upon
see how he goes from one to another
loving and leaving
heartless as any

What do you see of me? he said
Is it my fancy garments that so attract you?

But this I promise, that if your love is True
    then I can never leave you

GOPIKA-VALLABHAM

How can I leave You
when You've been everything to me?

Through countless creations
    You've been my Everything

We've played every relationship,
loved and hated, cried and laughed

I remember You
    as I remember my own self

What madness is it that I can leave You
when You've been Everything to me

The one who answered my forgotten prayers
    crowned my life
made worthwhile all Existence
    proved all poetry
washed me out in Himself

It is only by Your Unbound Grace
that I now know
    that you have always been
        My All

MURARI

When you meet Him in that final place
the Dark One will ask:
>   *Do you want the things of the world
>   or do you want immortality?*

And there, amidst all the demons of
lust, greed, power, vanity
 that stand and watch,
you must make your choice

Will you leave Him waiting

or will you overcome yourself
        and the world

CHITTA-CHORA

Could his name be enough?

Would his smile in the heart be too much?

Devotion

MY MASTER

With You it was not love at first sight
        but the first sight of Love

With You it is was not
when You looked in my eyes
        but when You became my sight

With You it is not when you see me
        but when You see me Seeing

that I know I've loved You
before time began

DEVOID

Devotion—
Not what it seems
Not sweet words and praise
but a giving up of yourself again and again
so that Truth wins each time

Not a determined loyalty
but an endless steadfastness to Silence

Not a lazy surrender to a form where you're
tempted to glance out of the corner of
      your eye for a reaction
But a surrender of all knowledge
that leaves not a single tool in your hand

Devotion
is loving Krishna as Radha

Silence
is knowing that Krishna himself is Radha
and Radha
      is only another Krishna

BREATHED

Let me not think that my eyes saw
Let me not think that my ears heard
or that my lips spoke ever a word

Every breath that came as life
bringing fears and joys
tears laughed and cried—
Let not me ever imagine
that it wasn't your breath that breathed me

FOR THE LOVE OF GOD:

May my gratitude be pure—
the only thing I can offer You

O Lord who can grasp your mysteries:
I cannot claim any victories
I cannot even claim surrender

To whom will you confide O heart?
At every corner runs a circus here
Who is the special one to whom you'll
pour yourself out?
Which one looks most like God?

When the times comes
that the tide of God reaches you,
              will you drop your oars
          and let the ocean carry your boat?

HeartWords

        yours is no-one
        yours is only God

Devotion

My eyes are tired from looking at the world
Will you give me a new world O Lord
or will you give me new eyes?

O Lord
trap me
inside the cage of your heart
In that cage is my freedom

God says:
Every moment I'm loving you
but you don't see...
because in every moment
I'm loving you
in a new way
and you deny
my Infiniteness

See with your real eyes
your true eyes
the eyes of God

Devotion

True, living devotion
as if to fall
could be Grace
and to resolve—
might disrespect a sacred freedom

O my Lord
tell me true
if I have ever wanted anything but You
Even if it appeared
like I wanted something other
was it not only because I mistook it for You?

If I fail in my duties
let them know
I was distracted by God

Some things are between you and God
until all things are between you and God

HEARTWORDS:

What madness is it that I forget
    that I've been waiting for You?
What madness is it that I don't remember
    my prayers while You're answering them?
What madness is it that I don't realise
    how madly I've always been in love with
                                       You

Hidden from idle looks
* Yet never not here*

Devotion

Sometimes I leave you in time
but if I leave time
I never leave You

Take your eyes off the world
Take your eyes off the world
Take your eyes off the world

ONE

Who is it that looks out
at your eternal incompleteness in form
the eternal grasping
in an endless universe
never to be fulfilled...
for to fulfil would be to
bring something to end
and God's being is endless

Who looks?
Is it not the Completeness
the ever-fulfilled-ness-
the One
and only

FORGOTTEN

If you believe something in what happens can
give you happiness
then you'd never choose to be that quiet one
in the back of the room
who got left out of all the conversation
but in whom God so fully shines

TO KNOW HIM:

Find the greatest in yourself
the purest feeling
the good-est you've felt
Love—even if the barest hint
and keep choosing it
every moment

Like this you tune yourself
to God's rhythm

You wake up to see a world
of innumerable forms
all reflecting Him
all pointing back
at your awakeness

Devotion

Something must become so drenched
and soaked
that there is no place for anything else
in the infinite space

Live in love with God
Live in Love, with God

Devotion

All ask God for so many things
but isn't it funny, ironic and true:

that I ask and ask
when I see you as name and form

but when I see you as God
I want nothing from you

MY MASTER

Master, I use everything of yours

Through your eyes I see
through your knowledge I know
through your wisdom I understand
through your love I shine

I use your powers to transcend
      Even the earnestness is yours

Sometimes I see Krishna in your eyes
Sometimes I feel Shiva in your presence
Sometimes I see Christ in your smile

All times
I hear the Universe in your words—
      spoken and unspoken

THE GURU

I staked my life on your every word
not having a clue where they led
but because I knew they came from Him
and I remembered
that He always spoke like that

So I couldn't help but stake my life
on your every word
The ones you spoke—
and those you didn't

IT IS ENOUGH

One drop of You is enough, Lord
my beggar mind will never understand
Your great abundance
that doesn't even know itself
That even when everything is taken
shines the One source of unending life
    whose innocence doesn't know its own
        purity
    whose fragrance is Beauty
    whose radiance breathes limitless Love

That Glorious One—
                one drop of whom is enough

Shiva

Shiva

THE UNKNOWN:

Every moment I am Shiva
Every moment I am death
Every moment I am life
Every moment I give all away
and get all back
Every moment I ebb
Every moment I flow
Every moment I know

Or maybe I do not know

How much Beauty I saw
standing on the edge of the cliff
Open to fall
Open to be saved
Open to die
or to live

How achingly beautiful it is
living forever on the edge
not knowing which side is life, which death
Surrendering all knowing
to That which dances
to an unstruck beat
who maybe also
doesn't know

Shiva

All my offerings don't please Him
my words of love don't impress
my tears don't move

I see why—
for Him
the whole world is late

I followed you to the end
hungry to know you
I went through you
through and through
and found only myself

DISSOLUTION:

O Shiva
destroy me in You!

Or do what You will
who am I
to tell You what to do

Shiva

In you is a love
where all the universes
come to dissolve

Om Namah Shivaya

That Shiva
That One
That has washed me out,
    taken all
and left me
    Without
so much—

He's taking my every breath

Shiva

What a spell You've cast on me
You've made me a slave with Your one touch

Beware all you who seek this Shiva:
when you invite Him to your house
He'll take All of you

HeartWords

The One I love—
He doesn't want the things I offer
All I offer, He burns to ash
    Cruel is the One I love—
He doesn't want to know me
Will I not then just slowly forget myself?
    How unkind is the One I love!
He doesn't want the parts of myself
that I give so freely—
    He wants All of me

THE GURU, THE BELOVED

What a sly one you are
invading without permission
Who said you could take every cell
and every thought
and turn it into your own?

I was waiting to rise, how naive!
    Your plan was an endless fall...

Still like a fool I earnestly pray
that in any realm of time or space
      wherever there's a 'coming' and 'going'
      and wherever there's a 'you' and 'me':

May I never come without you—
          May you never leave without me

ARUNACHALAM:

O Arunachala, all your forms don't fool me
They're just to test me, don't I know it?
As if I would not recognise you
if you came like this or that

When first ever I asked 'Who am I'?
I saw you standing Still
The Self is Silent, ever-present Answering
The mind goes round the hill

Shiva

What compliant
can I have
against the one
that is making everything dance?

*I tried to run away from You
but how to run away from one who is everywhere?*

If someone was telling
the secret of the universe,
would you listen?

He's telling it all the time

YOGESHWARAYA

Let the Shiva in you
destroy your world of meanings
of better and worse
of preferred and not
of beautiful and ugly
of joy and sorrow
of hate and love
of things and people

When all this is destroyed
only then have you freed
yourself of this world

MAHADEVA

They say you are love
You are not
They say you are compassion
You are not
You are the Ultimate end—

    You are Shiva

They say you speak the sweetest things
but you don't speak at all
They say you are the most loving
but you do nothing at all—

    You are only Shiva

They say you are the most righteous
but they don't see your tricks
They say you give liberation
but you trap them in your Stillness
Playing like Krishna, but really

    You are Shiva

Shiva

They say you show the way
but you only show a mirror
They say you help all
but you're only Here

> *Only life*
> *You are*
> *Shiva*

Veil Nebula

SHIVA-SHAKTI

I am the ever changing
and the ever unchanging
Madly in love with each other

Om Shiva Shakti

SHAMBHO

Tired of defiling you with words
Tired of defining you with worlds
I'd rather be your *Quietness*

Tired of studying your rhythm
Tired of learning your moves
I'd rather be your *Dance*

Tired of guessing your possibilities
Tired of imagining your impossibilities
I'd rather be what *Is*

Love

ALL OR NOTHING

What good is my love for you
if I don't hear you as the notes of music
or feel you as the evening breeze

what kind of Beloved would you be
if you didn't show your face in every cloud
or leave your fragrance in the trees

what would be the sense in loving you
if the stars didn't start to remind me of your eyes
and your smile was not the rising of the moon

what kind of love would it be
if you didn't become the world for me

what a waste of time to love You
if our Love still left us as two

VOICE OF LOVE

The voice of Love
makes the spring sing
    makes the brooks tinkle
    the ocean roar
    and the apple tree grow

That voice of Love spoke to me today
    and I overcame myself

YOU, LOVE

In your eyes
I see where the stars come from
    why the sun was born
and where the sky gets its endlessness from

In your voice
I hear the birds singing
the streams dancing
and the waves kissing the shore
                  in unending reunions

In your Love
I feel
    All Dissolve

GRACED

One who is drunk on the words of the *SatGuru*
how can he find anything in this world
interesting?

Intoxicated beyond care
        on the wine pouring from the Master's lips

Stoned on the Silence of the Divine

Love

MECHANICS OF LOVE

By letting you be exactly as you are
I free myself of you

How wonderful that by letting you go
I get more of myself back

And only then can I fully love you
for there's more of me to love you with

As I become me
you become me
all becomes Love
and the world falls quietly away

UN-BELIEVED

Heart-breaking beauty

Love
unexplainable

If it's not you...

then what you are, I know not

for what you want me to believe of you
I made unknowable to myself

ALL HERE NOW

All my love for you
is all my love for you Now

I don't save some love
for you for tomorrow
I don't save some love
for what you were yesterday

I thought that
if I spread out my love for you
over time
over happenings
over you
that it would be more

But then when you're here with me
Now
how can I hold back any of it?

All my love for you
is all my love for you
Now

HeartWords

TRUE LOVE:

                Sometimes there's Love
              Sometimes there's Silence

                 Expressing what's true:

                  the Silence of Love
              and the Love of Silence

Love

The most auspicious gift
I ever found to be true:

You were already in love with me
before I fell in love with You

So what if I forgot
to say 'I love you'
for a day or two

in a love affair
that has gone on
lifetimes

To be in love with you
is hard work
but to be Love with you
is effortless

Love doesn't come from stories
                    stories come out of Love

Love will make you walk a hard path
It will not stop until every bit of you
that you hold to save yourself
is cast in the fire
so that you have nothing to rely on
but Love

It's not because you're special
that I love you
but because you're the most ordinary
the most simple
for then I find that I fit fully into you
and lose all sense of difference

Love

when it is enough
it is Love

O what a blessed thing to see—
 the one I loved
  was only me

Thank you for letting me love you
so I can see where I am
and where you are not
and wipe off my existence
in the Love
that knows no otherness

HeartWords

I take you already
to be my most intimate lover
for I know you cannot live without me

                In my mind I make you
                     like a painting
                on an empty canvas

It became too painful to say 'I love you'
keeping always a two
High maintenance it was
this love for 'you'

So I did away with 'you'
by doing away with myself too

To be willing to leave your questions unanswered
that is Love
to be willing to be left hanging
to lose
is Love

*I don't call it Love
which can even for a moment
be apart from me*

Love

Only when I make you infinite
can I truly love you

*Otherwise you're just something
that hid infinity from me*

You said if I keep loving you
I will get nothing

I said that's okay
maybe that's what I've always wanted—
Nothing

Love

The truest love is never spoken about
The most precious thing, never shared

There may never have been a poet
that didn't keep the most cherished to herself

Life

SONG OF THE HEART

There is a song being sung
No-one knows where it started
or where it will end

Sometimes it feels off-key
but that's just improvisation
(like in jazz music)

In moments of total humility
faint strains are heard
      and the world is seen dancing
      on the notes of a flute

MY SHARING

What I want is to sing to you

      with intention, with agenda,
      with a will to teach or show
        much can come
            but poetry cannot come
            music cannot come

And what I want is for us to dance—

so we must become children again
when our knowledge didn't create
a higher and lower
and sunshine cleaned up after us always
      letting all be an innocent pretence

Life

SHAKTI

Sometimes you shine in spontaneous action
Sometimes in deliberate planning
In waiting and in non-waiting
From you arises devotion
You give the taste of wisdom
and the tastes of the tongue
A breath of air to support my life
A place to rest my head
Earth
Water
Heat
In Space my life is held
and nourished by your Love
O Mother
That came in the form of my own mother
to give a taste of mothering
How much more infinite is your care...
My speech couldn't come
if gravity didn't work or orbits strayed
and if a billion stars didn't rest content in
your care,
I couldn't have this moment with you today

INNOCENCE:

My seven year old eyes
saw only sunshine and joy

How is it then
that so much world got in the way

Life

Child of six, lying on the grass
eyes filled with light
Maybe the sun's, maybe not

The world appeared in sunshine, I thought
And all that world could disappear
    and I wouldn't notice

Seeing with new eyes now I know
that Light is not the sun's

It fills so completely all that appears
that all I called myself could disappear

    and I wouldn't notice

Effortless as the sunshine
free as the breeze
    Can't think your way to Wisdom
    Can't feel your way to Love…

                Why not, for once—
        let life have its way with you

ALL & I

The waves move shyly
>just like me
The clouds scurry about the sky—
>I am like that sometimes
The buds hesitate to take the next step;
>I see myself in that
The wind restlessly shifts…
>reminding me of myself
The stream laughs its head off
>just like me

We are the same—
>All and I

ALONENESS

stay alone
mature
find your unique flavour
every plant grows independently
and the garden blooms

The mind is telling stories
The heart is singing a song

SPECIAL

Life picked me up and crowned me
and I felt so special
but when it dismantled me
down to my atoms
and threw them to mix
with the atoms of all the universe
only then did I realise
how truly special I was

AUTUMN

If this warmth of the autumn light
is not a madness
If it is not crazy to watch the sky
without anything wanted
If it is not true that what you just spoke
came from a billion years ago
                    (just like stardust)
    Then I'm not sure what's true…

SUMMER

I love it when the sun kisses me
Such unabashed fondness!
The romantic tickle subsides after a while
but I can't get rid of the madness

WISDOM

Wisdom is in the moment
When we appropriate it
we believe we have to hold onto it
and we miss that more and more
and greater and greater
is always coming—
from this moment

Being true to Life
means a constant surrendering of our ideas
to this moment
so that it can reveal itself
and flow
in all the glory
of its intuitive wisdom

LIVING INFINITELY

Life, a beautiful contradiction
Letting go and holding on
Not knowing what to trust
and then fully trusting one thing
                         ...and everything

Allowing life to guide,
with a deep trust in oneself
to the exclusion of all else
    of others, social norms and rules
    of human direction altogether

An ever discrimination
    breathing
every half-moment by half-moment

An infinite surrender
—into eternity

A deep listening for life's pulse
in every moment

like an artist moulding her expression
submitting the flood of love and joy
to the hand of beauty and wisdom

Life

Looking for the signs from life in its wholeness

A human surrender lazily submits
but a true surrender walks bravely
through the Fire of Love
making everything (people, situations, ideas)
Infinite in its wake—

QUIET:

sit Still
    All that is meant for you
    will come to you
harmonize yourself
with the Mother of the universe
let Her Will abide

Life

Become as silent as a tiny leaf
pushed down by a raindrop
and up by the wind

SEARCH FOR AN ABSENCE

Art releases Beauty
because you lose some of yourself
in every bit of it
and so have a chance
of glimpsing the Universal

THE ARTIST

What artist ever sang her song well
with one eye on the listener?
Pay the price—*become the song*

The best art comes from a place of total loss
the highest joys forgotten
the hidden hurts relinquished
so that whatever remains may speak

See the greatest artist how He created
such unfathomable beauty
      Can anyone find Him
         or even His trace?

A GIFT

What was promised?
That one day these lips would start singing?
That the eyes would become filled with colour?
That something like a sound could emerge?
That something like a breath could come—
like a gift from Silence

> Close your eyes, my love
> so you can be shown in ways
> you could not see

ANCIENT PRAYER

We don't know how it is all working

Sometimes He raises one and lowers the other

Sometimes your harsh words burn the false
in another

Sometimes your anger makes a star
blink in the sky

Sometimes your smile came from the waterlilies
gifted upon a breeze

Sometimes the full moon needed your past pains
to become whole

Sometimes what was felt through your skin
was just what the whole universe had been
waiting for

You, each one,
         is the answer to an ancient prayer

May in this life, you find yourself with those
    who know in their hearts
        that they prayed for you

ALLOWED

Let it be a disappointment
Let it be not good enough
Let it be unfair
Let it be ugly
Let it fail you
Let it let you down
Let it be wrong

And show me where the sun stopped shining
and you stopped being
a child of God

EXPRESSION:

What comes to you without a 'should I'
or 'should I not'?
Something you can't help
Like when you are in love...?

A force cutting through your 'yes' and 'no'
Leaving you helpless....
That's your song to sing

Only in magic will you know

whatever comes from a thrilled heart
do
whatever makes the heart sing
do

A question brings death to the mind
when the answer is Life

LIFE'S ROMANTICISM

It's a romantic Heart at play

Waiting for that one word to set you free
Believing that a touch
will alchemically turn you into love
Trusting your next breath

Hoping...

If it is not the work of a crazy romantic

FALLING INTO SILENT STEP

Such a deep "being there" for Life...
as if to hold even the slightest ground for oneself
to stray for a half-moment even
would betray the Beloved
for you stopped listening to speak

Interrupted your Beloved's love song
to remind Him about the dishes

Even though only He ever interrupted
and only He ever listened—
to Himself

PERVADED

Gossiping in all the forms
playing as this and that

neither are the words of a poet great
nor the chirp of crickets mundane

COMPASSION

Your Compassion
is where you allowed life to show

Letting go the tight hold
on the suffering you want corrected
the unfairness that went unnoticed
the pain that burned
as if for a thousand years
If dropped, what a loss!
The injustice tears through the stomach

But look, what I saw—
I let go and life could breathe again
and danced in glorious wisdom
showing where I took a wrong view
opening other windows
so I could see more and more:

The one I looked to for approval—
a lost child needing mine

The one who blamed me—
stumbling in the darkness of time

Life

The gift of compassion, life left at my door
when I stopped stifling its show
saying instead, 'yes Life, I allow you to be'

in all your luxuries and your ditches,
your leafy-earthy breezes and your stenches
your celebrations and your brokenness

I allow you to unfold as me

HUMOUR

Kindness goes where logic cannot go
Love goes where kindness cannot go
Humour goes where love cannot go

Kind words, a loving hand...
but somehow it seems nothing can touch that
dimension of human connection
that humour does
Perhaps that is why it is the most incorruptible,
the least fake-able

Kindness says:
I know you need me and I'm here;
Love says:
I want to show you what's in myself so you'll find
it in yourself too
But when we laugh with someone,
there's no-one giving or receiving
Pure equality. Pure sharing.
Laughter says:
you don't need anything and I know that
And somewhere, deep down,
we both know that we're just fooling around

Life

The miraculous compassion—
even with all the wrong moves
Still
always in the right place

BY THEIR FRUITS ...

A fineness
an etiquette
a nobility
an elegance
A gentle fragrance clings...
the invisible crown gifted by Her
when you forgot to ask
what do I have to show for it?

By their fruits you will know them

TIMELESS

My name is not in language
My age is not in time

I don't even know I am

When time stops
I am still here

When time starts
there is no start in Me

CHOICE

Yes, there's a deep hurt
Yes, it's been unjust
Yes, it's not fair
Yes, it's not right
Yes, you wish you could change it

But see how a baby is born into this world
with fresh eyes
Would you like to tell her how bad this world has been to you?
What would you like to tell this baby about this world?
Choose —
because you can

Tell her that this world has a beautiful sky
where fluffy white clouds play
and so many creatures and plants, colours and smells, flowers and people of all kinds,
that you'll never be able to know it all

Maybe if you get to see a sea or two
    you'll be one of the lucky ones
who got to fill their toenails with wet sand

Life

And don't forget to feel the sun on your closed eyelids
especially in the morning when the breeze is cool

And there are tears and fears
    and joys and laughs here
but nothing stays
    So when they're here,
don't forget to love them with all your heart

And don't forget to listen for the music

You can sing and dance to it
or you can simply close your eyes and feel
    that the whole world
is only the music of your being

HEART OF NATURE

We came to see with sunlit eyes
touch soft petals in the morning light
Merge breath with wind
Fragrant delight
and a subtle song
resting deep inside
a baby bud

Life

WATERFALL

A drop falls
and along with it,
the entire water-
Falls
Smashing upon cool earthy stone

wet feet,
breath of mud and forest leaves

And my heart beams knowing
I am all I ever knew

Freedom

FREEDOM SONG

The great Masters are singing a song
Declaring is uncooth
but feeding what's known back to the Source
releases a song so sweet
that the mind,
not being called to agree or submit
simply yields

It's singing through all the hearts
— All the time

OF IDENTITY

You want to be lifted out
from where you think you are

O
my
Love

Let me go tell the whole Universe
so it can lift you up
to your unbounded Heart
so you remember that yours is the power
that goes from the roots in the earth
to the space-dust scattered across the milky ways
Whether a billion years old or yet to come
makes no difference
to you who's neither before nor after

FREEDOM DANCING:

>
> Freedom is the one
> that knows
> how to dance
> with every atom
> of the universe.

My freedom
is that I don't have to conclude
I don't have to say yes or no
I don't have to like or hate
I don't have to be this or that

Nothing compels to make a stand
All can move like desert sands

Freedom

Nothing true
needs to be asserted

The truest love,
never spoken of

The greatest joys,
left dancing on silent lips

Silence:

holding the murmurings of sweet-nothings
and the explosions birthing galaxies
with equal ease

SOMETHING ELSE ALTOGETHER

What void are you trying to fill
by wanting from the appearance?

Come my love
    rest and see

It is something else
that doesn't want

don't look, don't find

It is something else…

LEAVE

Can you leave everything
unresolved
unconcluded
no final judgment
no finale´
no ending

Quiet
Motionless

Step out
without even taking a step

WHO AM I

Who Am I?

Am I a person feeling hard done by
    or am I the waves frothing on the beach

Am I the one you forgot about
    or am I the sunlight streaming through
    the trees

Am I the one who lost
    or am I the birds on a summer breeze

Am I the one always waiting
    or am I the one who thought up time itself

RE-EMBRACE

A total freedom
so that even the minutest gasp of air
must be the Beloved
and every particle of dust
floating in the sunlight

If finding her as Silence
meant you lost all words for a while
All dissolved, both the joys and pain

And when you come to speak again
it's of the commonest things—
dust and groceries and curtains
and orange peels…
It's because you fell in love with life again

BLACK HOLE

Turned in on itself
into an endless falling

Emptied out at centre
and re-filled with power

Galaxies dancing round

You're so Great...

Splendour spills

        and you argue about lights and sounds

*Looking for freedom I came
and became the ultimate slave*

On writing

As a child, I'd discovered something mystical about words. I found that if I really sat with them, feeling them truly and fully, I would go through them to a space of sunshine and peace. A place of temporary disappearance; where the world was squared away. Then every word that came to be written felt holy and I'd never feel to change anything written.

The best words and any art seem to come from a churning that left no tangible trace but still, a knowing is shared in invisible ways that something was lost…and maybe something found.

To crack open words, to make them lose their rigidity and right-ness. To make them dance and sing, needs a poking, a chopping, a twisting and turning.

Somehow only then do things come to life.
A wrestling with something 'imposed' to sing a fresh song into it. Burning what's known and

seeing where life might choose to burst forth through it.

The most enjoyable writing is when there is enough leeway for the reader to join the writer in completing the sentences. Where language is not just utilitarian but more true to its essence in being a shared experience where both sides willingly step into intimacy. Where the other implicitly agrees to drop their resistance by playing as if it was your words they enjoyed, when really it was the essence of their own self.

- ecstatic dance ✗
- urban retreat ✗
- SS full day ✗
- SS ½ day ✓
- lunch ??? ✓
- dinner ✓
- music ✓
- mother mary ✗
- pouch ✓
- diffusers n ting ✓
- shamans ✗   coin ✓

Sunday plans? x

Printed in Great Britain
by Amazon